Rags of My Soul

"Not even when life's last ray
Has fled does every ill depart, nor all
Corporeal taints quite leave their unhappy frames.   (920)
And needs must be that many a hardened fault
Inheres in wondrous ways. Therefore the pains
Of punishment they undergo, for sins
Of former times. Some in the winds are hung
Suspended and exposed. Others beneath   (925)
A waste of waters from their guilt are cleansed,
Or purified by fire."

Vergil, *The Aeneid*, Book VI
(Trans. by Christopher Pearse Cranch)

Rags of My Soul

Poems

T. Byram Karasu

ROWMAN & LITTLEFIELD PUBLISHERS, INC.
Lanham • Boulder • New York • Toronto • Plymouth, UK

ROWMAN & LITTLEFIELD PUBLISHERS, INC.

Published in the United States of America
by Rowman & Littlefield Publishers, Inc.
A wholly owned subsidiary of The Rowman & Littlefield Publishing
Group, Inc.
4501 Forbes Boulevard, Suite 200, Lanham, Maryland 20706
www.rowmanlittlefield.com

Estover Road
Plymouth PL6 7PY
United Kingdom

Distributed by National Book Network

British Library Cataloguing in Publication Information Available

Library of Congress Cataloging-in-Publication Data

Karasu, Toksoz B.
  Rags of my soul : poems / T. Byram Karasu.
     p. cm.
  ISBN-13: 978-0-7425-6381-0 (cloth : alk. paper)
  ISBN-10: 0-7425-6381-2 (cloth : alk. paper)
  ISBN-13: 978-0-7425-6466-4 (electronic)
  ISBN-10: 0-7425-6466-5 (electronic)
  I. Title.
  PS3611.A7773R34 2009
  811'.6—dc22   2008030313

Printed in the United States of America

The Aeneid, Book Six, by Vergil, translated by Christopher Pearse Cranch,
courtesy of Barnes & Noble, Inc.

The Aeneid, Book Six, by Virgil, translated by David West (Penguin Books,
1990). Introduction and translation copyright (c) David West, 1990.

"Book Six: The Kingdom of the Dead," from VIRGIL: *THE AENEID* by Virgil,
translated by Robert Eagles, copyright (c) 2006 by Robert Eagles. Used by
permission of Viking Penguin, a division of Penguin Group (USA) Inc.

Contents

Part I

THE SCARS OF AN UNSUBSTANTIATED LIFE

"Aeneas . . . asked . . .
what was that river in the distance and who were all those   (710)
companies of men crowding its banks. 'These are the souls to
whom Fate owes a second body,' replied Anchises. 'They come
to the waves of the river Lethe and drink the waters of serenity
and draughts of long oblivion'"

Virgil, *The Aeneid*, Book VI
(Trans. by David West)

The Scars of an Unsubstantiated Life

If you accept my discontent and not just my intemperance,
My "rages" and "counterfeit glooms,"
Our life would run its similitude course;
Hard silence, tedious dances, and mutual upbraidings.
If you accept
My "profane" right to be exempt from the rules of life—
Unfaithful to myself—
Our life would run its undaunted course;
No apologies, no reconciliations, or worse, feigned submis-
    sions,
A taste of vengeance.
If you accept my exile from myself and not just my abortive
    life,
Our life would run its un-melodious course,

If you accept my travels of sin proceeded with harm to
All—most to myself—reinventing death as endless punish-
   ment,
Fiercer by despair,
Our life would run its corrosive course, as not to secure
Any expiable hate from roughest tongues,
Proved pernicious.

Disappropriation

Do I know any better who I am? Or only
Feigning just to arm myself against
Time's accusations; after all
I have promises to keep: move out
Of my anxious home and forgive all
My peripheral wrongs—wrong for my years.
I'll tell the truth for once, leave enough
Unsaid and tear up all warrants.

I thought eventually nothing will be left
At the edges of the light and I'll be transparent in
Dark labyrinths. There'll be neither
Wrong nor right, nor dissenting noises.

Now all these bear revisions, for I found
An unretrieved claim in a well of
Bitter tears: A new warrant.
I don't remember anything I confessed. Yes,

I don't know any better who I am. I came
To deign innocence—a longing
In vain. All seems to be lost on me; even
The despair is no longer my own.

Even Ever

If I ever loved before, I didn't. The thing,
Resembled broodings of its tribulations.
On the far side of ungirdled, and quiverings
Of garish desires—for whatever reason
Bearing the name of love.
I tried to decipher myself, trapped in
Silences of mortal stakes, but still
Hauled in salt and sweat of errors
Never to be scaled.

If I even love today, I don't. The unthing
Resembles fleetings of its deliverance.
On the near side of tears;
Wrinkled and dissonant.
I tried to remember myself, distracted in
Silences of the gnawing facts, but still
The song and dance of terrors—deathless
Must remain untold.

Love and Death

I have been waiting for this moment to inform you, love
Is a feast of pain and loneliness, wrapped in erratic
Wilderness; weaving your grave into a cold and hallowed
Ground; it is a brutal unrest, in full view of indifferent
Glares, plucked from coiling lies, vainly seeking the
Nuptial song. Love is a sexual drift, the clumsiest disguise
Of narcissism; a few orgasmic trickles, a dust to sight,
    a prelude
To plaintive and misshapen whine;
    an unexacting spawn
Of feelings, feeding an infantile lack of balance. Love
Is a guilty stare of fears and an intransigent quest for hate;
An old celestial order, a curse of time, like death.

Some of These

In the beginning was the Deed
The time was slain
Irrevocably, and
Framed for the covenance
All desecrations were rendered sinless
God was pregnant
I remember yet
More than all of these

We plunged into a dark void
Howling our nowhereness
Perilous descent, and
Destined for unholy lost
God was yawning
I remember yet
Less than all of these

At the end was a massive silence
The earth was stripped bare
And crucified
Into a void—
God was in mutation—
I remember yet
None of these

Interred Longing

At the oddest moments—times of
Fierce intimacy.
You're absolving my empty feat:
"I shall not love."
You're imputing my endless breach
In a furtive vein;
Draining your sad patience
Into my virtuous lies;
You're framing my semblance of self
Replete with the worst of wrongs, within
A love bearing quietude. Not that
We had no bonds of love or
Lust;
But the time decayed my venoms,
Now, all seems withering
In my interred longing.

Half-concealed

How should it begin?
"A heap of the squandered!"
Too harsh a cadence.
In final lingerings to
Far off melodies?
Hardly responsive to absent kisses?
No longer tortured by any desire?
Half concealed.
Unremittingly aimless?
Almost the life itself—
The meaning expunged and erased, and
Lost, above all, the struggle
Against time.
Come then, to find some ease in
The uncertainties of
No divine origin.

Turns of Life

The last I saw was her stare
Sentencing me
Behind darkened walls,
Hell-bent in her
Muted voice—
Plunging me to depths of
Inward wrath;
She assailed my past
Feverless silence
My promises
Within narrow bounds
What was it?
Pangs of old devotion
Could it be so easily lost
In a turn of life?

Perverse Joy

All this was a long time ago
There was a man, a force to yield
In sullied frame;
He was not taught of fear
Or wrong;
No one dared to imitate
His natural vices.
He had a mind
Ruthless and untamed,
Received many wounds
Outstripped death;
He was impervious to innocence
Deep-rooted in time,
His deliberate unhappiness—
Perversely joyful—
Sentenced him
To himself.

The Carcass of Love

If this is the end, then
In the self-blaming simplicity
I would like to render right
And yield to my fate
Spinning still
Without pangs of doubt or
Tribulations;
Petrify
In the names of frowning gods
Till no trace is left from
The carcass of our love.

Forgiveness

Tell me if I am a loser
As a lover,
Then there will be nothing more to say or spend
Seismic emotions.
Tell me if I am emptied out of passion and
Poetry;
Battered fugitive from love
Being all unfit;
If my love is
The harbinger of all wrongs
Sequestered in its own wrath and
Still clinging
To your shrine.

Your Unwavering Mind

Let us try again
Leave nothing unsaid—
A linear course—
I'll listen unsheltered,
Not weigh you down
With my ambushes or
Decaying wits;
I'll not sink to worn out
Display of unhappy wounds
In the maze of
Frugal tales;
I'll not invoke the infrangible
In my beating the light, but still
I will remain treacherously
In your mind.

Deities of Love

I was young and light
Not yet undone
An unresisting prey to
Profane violence
Many a wound.
I was too precise
Stranger to riddles and
Female beds
They asked me to love them
Scarcely understood,
Deities of love.
I may err on this, but
It was not an easy thing to do
Uncharted senses
What did they really want?
Unaware of the privilege of dissolution
Turned adrift
Now, I sang their pain.

The Truthless Mind

There was a girl of a hot summer
Without provenance, who
Plundered my world, simply
With some kind of laughter—
Lies concealed within.
She lured me and a few others to
Her frozen bed, then
Blotted all of us out, cureless—
No traces of regret.
Yet I confess she puzzled me—
A truthless mind—
Does love die in fearful angst
Or in cynical despair?

The Abuse of Time

Why do I long for endless life
At the oddest moments of
Never nothing—
Where hovers
The now; in
Unknown forms,
Strung together with
Unmeant cadence;
All things hewned and left
Empty of bashful shapes;
I long for a hiding place
Fastened to
Amniotic patience,
While I abuse my time.

Ecstatic Confusion

It is painfully true:
The wet odor and
Shades of your sweat
Have broken the spell;
Your touch—undiluted and bland—
Sealed the darkness
Of my romantic worship; and
Finally slayed
My last impulse.

Crucified into Love

Held a few
Spasms of sex
"Do you love me?"
She asked again,
In the shade of her breath.
I am worn out, from
Indeterminate emotions
And deeds;
Sustained no loss, but
Just the same
Crucified into love.

Unhappiness

As to my unhappiness
First I thought
It wasn't my own—
An alien emotional voice—but then
It staggered in
With anxious power,
And cobwebbed into my mind
In slow mutation;
Stripped it bare of hopes and
Drank my light;
Howled my nowhereness
Fulfilling life's—my own—
Nothingness

Love without Object

I could stop, right now, living
Death had already kissed my breath
Twice;
Or I could just drift,
Fate had been braided into my life
Triple;
Adopt the paradigm of ache of being
"Loved and left;"
Embark on believing in
Instinct-driven temples,
Built by man,
And be faith-smitten;
Fearfully meditate gods—
Hope and gloom—
Defy my existence in
The infinity of time and then
Fall from heaven to earth,
To acquire love
Without object—
While all things speak of none.

Litters of Innocents

Loves made of nights
Precipitate in
Fate of synthetic halos;
The lips of the darkness
Thick as unforgiven
Lower their sights;
Poor in atonement
Deprive deep their
Spilled souls in
Bare vagueness;
In a pulse of a thunder
Of less and less
Keep littering the innocence
Before the meaning takes over
That has come and gone,
Then nothing happens.

A Vague Regret

What is exactly between us?
Tearing each other to shreds—
Breath to breath—
Till nothing remains, except
Broken sounds of
Discordant cries.
Still drooling blood and
Feeling a strange high
Only the need to forget
In a flare of time
A vague regret.

Far Removed

I have been thinking of our bruised life
Your fierce love, your nuptial kisses
Cadences of your laughter and
Their intransigent purpose:
Wooing to incinerate the ache of
My unmeant falseness.
Yet, you receive only plaintive spasms
Wrapped in diverse intent
The gnawing sense love
That holds you in orbit, only
Marks my limits
Far removed.

A Lingering Doubt

I thought I saw you again in
Half-deserted streets of Avenue C,
Sidled up to a tall frame—
It was trembling hours;
You looked in my direction
Indifferent, then,
Lighted a moment of kiss.
Should I then believe that
You once loved me? or
I no longer exist.

Knowing

I had never seen you, never smelled
Your voice; but I think I know you, because I
Believe in desire. You had never seen me,
Never heard my breath; but you think you know me
Because you believe in remorse.
When life had failed me,
I abandoned you and
All other shrines. You cleaved only to
Solitude, lulled your passion to sleep
Kindred emotions.
Had I been more careless and unaltered
My impulses, you might have dumped on me
The load of your virtual heart and
All other ruins from its own wreck;
Then may be then
We might not have really known each other.

Decomposer

Perhaps it is not too late turning
An inquiring gaze
To the forager of forbidden joys
Uncurbed;
To the stupor downward, molesting
The dignity of moral tempest
Unimpeded;
To the fearful, in a
Sigh—tuneless—
Lurking behind the tears
The zen-like defiler of soul
Meditated;
To the devourer of flesh
At the threshold of
Decomposition.

At the Core

Why does it trouble you that I have no stakes
In all worldly longings
Isn't that painfully obvious?
I am simply loitering, rudderless
Among the caskets of aborteds

Why do you want to dissemble my darkness?
I am all eyeless
Isn't that tedious?
I am just petitioning, clueless
In the realm of obscenity

Why does it scare you that I lay bare
All my secrets?
Isn't that tepidly useless?
I am simply steeped in slaying
Gods of polluted shrines.

The Fast and Furious

Do not disturb the order here, we are just fine
Undisguised scorns
We are here to laugh, sing, dance and lie
Disharmonious truths
Do not impose your ruefulness on our happy one
Conceit of sadness
We simply need streams of images
Intricate recesses
Don't inflict your gnawing on our lives
Perplexed chastisements
We are not interested in believing or not believing
No sadness in our eyes
Don't accuse us from
Loss of convictions
We need our gift of rage
Don't worry that one day it might burn us all
The ice flame
We need to live fast and furious
The folly of it

Bylaws of Love

There are laws of love. Uninformed, if not
Ignorant.
First of all, love is only bartered with love;
No rattling of the cage of sex then brutally offering
Clenched thighs.
No burning holes in all senses,
Then laying waste the garden, and litter it with
Idle tales.

There are simple rules of love. Uninterested, if not
Disdained.
First of all, no stirring with breathing voice, then
Deprive deep. This is not what is meant by never sown
Wild oats.

There are manners of love. Disregarded, if not
Trespassed.
First of all, don't smell fragrance of
Night, whisper faint noises, and then practice
Passionate disobedience.

There are codes of love. Disbelieved, if not
Surprised.
First of all, don't take everything personally
Nothing is meant by "I love you." Summary sentences
Are indented. These are only the sweet torments, the gentle
Art of hurting.

There are decrees of love. Negated, if not
Suffered.
First of all, no synthetic love follows the
Natural. Every love foresees its end in the lap
Of intransient wrongs. When there is nothing more to say,
Bathe in tears.

Out of Dust

You speak of hate that never failed,
I don't know how to disbelieve you;
You reduced us to scorn, pelt us with
Wisps of pain; but again,
Who dares to remember lastingness?
You mutter of lust that never sated,
I don't know how to relieve you;
You say my kisses are tentative
And outworn; of course,
What grows in darkness.

You speak of love that never failed,
I know why I shouldn't believe you;
There are showers of hail before the tempest,
Carnage and ruin after
Sadness; then again,
Even if the truth is stillborn and
Every thread is torn,
I know that I would recall you, even
Out of dust, because
I germinate in darkness.

Tender Empathy

I have submitted to a new emotion;
An emotion that dizzies me of thought—
Unmanageable and unruly.
Thoughts that store endless riddles and random
Craters—unbraided and vagrant—
Regaling only selfishness;
They harbor quarrels and are bent
On making my sleep fierce and dreamless, while
Rendering nothing back except terror
Smitten vagueness.
I have found a new emotion, an emotion
That never utters a word, though it can be heard;
That never shatters a moment, but
It renews the impediments.
I may as well be left to my hermitage
To obscure guilts, cheerless—
The throwback to
How I ought to feel.

Interpretation of Other

I tried to forget the last words
Uttered with a smile on your face
Impersonating despair
Your repose to my bewilderment—
Your disdain.

What is this stir to perish, yearning
To hear blackness sing, drowning all hymns
Weeping unwilling tears?
You wake up all my fears and self blames—
Your perdition.

How does one annul love?
You don't wince, though you offer
A few lipless kisses to
A famished mind
Is the love songless?
Dipped in your soul.

What is it like to be you, inexorable,
Armed with lack of pity, you hunt preys
Then thicken your blood—
Infinitesimal wounds in silence
No sense of wrong?

What if It Is Real?

Last night, I stood in a
Fragment of intent. A voice asked
"Head or tail?"; and offered to drink
Luke-warm tears of a young man;
Then pretended to mangle the head
Of an old woman in a frozen tomb. I was reticent
First, then guessed that this was a dream—
A harbinger of self-loathing. So I clung
  to my confession.
All the witnesses got up and
Left me in confusion. "Tail," I shouted.
Memories came flooding from ages long gone by.
"Your life is warped and overworn," the voice declared,
  "You'll be
Exiled to mute echoes, unfrequented
even with sleep."
I wanted to tell the story that repeats,
Without a respite

All seemed random, piled on my rehearsed crimes.
The voice drowned all other thoughts: "This is the day that
    you'll have
No remorse, but a lot of fear and despair;
Your wrongs are vague so too will be your punishment: Not
    wearing
The mask of guilt."

An Author

My whole life I lived in bizarre thoughts—
Fields of confusion—
Told stories of squalid minds
To endless strings of sobs;
I tied and untied innumerable knots
Of disorder of lies;
I have knocked at many doors,
Lashed open
Remnants of shouts,
And hoarded their lacerations.
I steeled myself to
The immunity of heart,
While love
Lagged behind.

Part II
FEAR OF LANDING

"The seeds of life—
fiery is their force, divine their birth, but they
are weighed down by the bodies' ills or dulled
by earthly limbs and flesh that's born for death.
That is the source of all men's fears and longings,
joys and sorrows, nor can they see the heavens' light,
shut up in the body's tomb, a prison dark and deep."

Virgil, *The Aeneid*,
Book VI, The Kingdom of the Dead
(Trans. by Robert Fagles)

Fear of Landing

What do you fear? You slip in and out
Of my space; dwell only to quiet your body and
Bruise my mind.
You turn ghostly just before each sunrise;
Is that because you have no desire but
The counterfeit heart—the unuttered—
Or because your gods are never at dawn?

What do you yearn for? You fall in and out
Of my moment; hoard only to fill your vault and
Empty my soul;
You smother me with flowers and hang me
Upon a kiss and cascading tears.
Is that because you are simply purging
Your pain—the shallow depths and the unutterable—
Or because your gods never loved?

What do you sing? You breathe in and out
Of my lungs; try only to weave your aloneness
Into my whole, and
You reduce me to smiles and blameless name;
Is that because you are neither close nor far from
The ground?—Unavailing voice and unencumbered—
Or because your gods never lived?

What do you pray? You dance in and out
Of my steps; return only, to perfect your sadness and
Satiate mine, and
You rapture and torment with your stinting love;
Is it because you are neither dead nor alive,
In the teeth of faith—be it false or true—
Or is that because your gods never died?

We All Wanted Her

There is a tale of a woman who drank
Songs, ate dances, and whispered invitation
With her summer moods.

She is said to melt mirrors, spill
Guilt, disturb minds, and lure others
With her face of love.

She would purge of sins, disrobe
Off thoughts, abandon the garden, and render all
Captive of senses.

She would wail out all sorrows,
And creep into man's soul with
The rhythm of a cradle.

She would rage, incinerate, confuse all
Wishes, offer a feast of pain and console
Within her womb.

She is said to have died with kisses on
Her eyes, the earth coiled, and the time dissolved
Left her skies weeping.

Farewell to Love

Is this the last kiss, for it seems
Exhales passion;
Lingering of phantom lips that
Exhume ruins.

Is this the last embrace, for it seems
Inhales regret;
Melancholy sobs that
Infuse tumult.

Is this the last sex, for it seems
Derails the sadness of farewell;
Elegy for tears, that
Seem devoid of desire.

I Don't Know What to Make of You

Of all the lips that I have kissed, I have
Mistaken yours, telling the truth.
I called it mocking; you barely
Disagreed.

Of all the pains that I have felt, I have
Dreaded the most, your countenance.
You called it vacant; I hardly
Believed.

Some said you were totally wild, if not crazy,
A lost soul, steeped inbred
Rage, lying hidden in your scaffold charm,
Undivided.

Others said you were brazen
An inmate of all devouring,
Frenzied love, dipped in the scent of blood,
Unindicted.

I don't really know what to make of it,
Of all the things everyone said;
A horrid truth lay upon my mind,
Uninvited.

The Snubbing Darkness

You may as well know this about me: it is
Simply my fate, to be
A survivor of too many menaces and
Their moods.

I am worn out of women's way of
Loving and my recklessness
To forget my being stripped bare
With their violence.

You don't want to hear, that I
Conspired with them to be ambushed
In an aching lust
With their delights.

I seem to be still alive but
Laid across, offering wounds—
Pulseless; showing marks of
Indiscriminate teeth.

You may as well know this about me:
Whoever beckoned me, I seeded; to be
Saved in their warm darkness
And that is not even the half of it.

Insignificance

I saw the stars steal the shadows
Of reluctant earth and
Anoint the gods
To the heaven's breast.

I saw the darkness sever the lights
Of sheltered earth and
Scatter the fleeting gods
To the sky's quest.

I saw the torrents impale
The immaculate earth and
Parody the yielding gods
To their fondling dome.

I saw the songlights caress
The sights on maculate earth and
Shelter the tenuous gods
To their mysterious prayers.

What Good Is It Now?

I was never told
Love is found and lost
Bittersweet profound;
Where the day recedes and the darkness roams,
I still thread the needle's eye in
Sorrowful hours;
Yet, I could have loved you.

I was never told
Time sinks the fire
In the loosened thighs, moribund;
Where the self secedes and the formless roams,
I still harbor in gasping shores
Tethered soul;
Yet, I could have loved you.

I was never told
Tears would blind man and
The embrace of woman's inside;
Where heaven descends and the boundless roams,
I still hover over the impulses hid—
Swelling on the ground;
Yet, I could have loved you.

Because You Have Loved Me

There is no time
I am suspended on the wind
I left my name behind
Because you have loved me

There is no space
I am grounded in stars
I left my home behind
Because you have loved me

There is no life
I am silenced in thoughts
I left myself behind
Because you have loved me

Tonal Nostalgia

The night was still, scaleless
The moon shimmering
Shrines were muted
Dissonance of time

The day was drunk, fleeting
The wind brooding dust
Utter dissolution
Ineffable tale of time

The night was short, suspended
Stars twinkling
Drifting into the precipice of lust
Twilight of time

The day was tainted, oblivious
Earth mourned
Where dwelled her ashes
Dissention of time

Beyond

I could never remember
Who thawed the story
With a scorching indignation;
Who muffled the silence
Beyond derision?
Who curved the colors
With a convincing incarnation;
Who frayed the essence
Beyond envision?
Who thorned the halos
Without breaking in pain
White carnations;
Who, in eternal hours
Beyond revision?

A Wobbly Ascension

In the beginning was the pilgrimage to
Tender atrocities
At the edge of unbending lights,
Nothing was itself.
Smiles crept into shadows of
Every emancipated evening; if that was not enough,
The original sin got reenacted, knocking
A hole in every unforgiving past,
Finally one too many; spilling
Into the noise of tears, waiting for the end.
Now, everything is itself, at the near edge of discontent,
As if plunged deep into abandon;
A resignation? No, a wobbly ascension.

Should I Then Believe?

Because I do not wish to hope again
To be near
An ill-disguised indifference
Should I then believe
My hurried life?
Because I do not wish to love again
To be nearer
An illusioned difference
Because I do not wish to die again
No nearer
A handful of dust
Should I then believe
My buried life?

Not That Easy

I could cite your tenderest lies,
Up to the last details—
Etched in my mind, but still
I don't know how to find you.
I could echo your sweetest truths,
Up to vanishing away—
Refused to leave my mind, but still,
I could lull your blessed spells—
Up to the final asunder—
Made, unmade my mind, but still
I don't know how to find you.
I could hush your stressed songs
Up to the contented surrender—
Trampled—to crush my mind, but still
I don't know how to find you.

Yes, It Was

There were years
Tale is told
Fiercest passions came forth
Impulses bear down;
Quivering lips
Uttering promises—
In whispered hymns.
Tell me it was true.
A frail longing endured
Coldest glares
Capturing the innocent wiles
As silence simmered
Puddle of tears—
Torturing the unwilling flesh.
Tell me it wasn't true.

Our Secret Must Never Be Known

We promised never to tell anyone
In tender vows
From this day forth
Till ensnared by
Errant hopes

We promised never to take refuge
In tangled knots
From this day forth
Till plundered by
Thoughtless songs

We promised never to look rueful
In vacant words
From this day forth
Till preyed upon by
Loveless souls and not so
Silent tears

I Loved Her, Isn't That Enough?

Once upon a time, there was a
Young girl;
Sun kissed her hair, boys
Her lips.
Did I know her?
I cannot say, only
Obscure reveries—
Brittle and sleepless.
I helplessly wandered into
Musical caresses and curvatures
Being wrapped in
Her delicate scorn;
The same impatience,
Mistakes and other familiar knots
Why does it always come to that?
I plunged into an empty well;
Failing and feeble—
I moved alone.

I cast my eyes upon the mystery of things
Blinded with tears;
The last thing I saw was
The darkness in light.
Did I really know her?
I cannot tell;
I loved her, isn't that enough?
Once upon a time, well
A bewildering tale.

Cavernous Ache

Again, the Spring never arrived—the reminiscence
Of all other fallacious hopes—as if there were
A broken link, in the chain of ancient times. But you
Seemed to be in your native element,
   unruffled woman—
Many winters of wrinkled promise: The sun will melt
The frozen eggs. But what if I poisoned them
With my gloom and my pine for
Obliterating cavernous longing?

Again, the meaning never arrived, the remembrance
Of all other endless choices; as if there were
A mutinous drift in the consciousness. But you
Subdued all debris of yearnings, unhesitant—the woman
Of many emblems—sealed regrets: the love will pelt
The self-haunting. But what if I hoarded them
With my chases and my time for
Premeditating disarrayed achings.

Let

God spoke: Let there be . . .
What?
Unbarred gates of immutables—
Perilous attempts;
Unimaginable lands of unrest—
Self-haunting;
Uninterdictable signs of ignorance—
Deigned infinite;
Unattainable light of darkness—
Fallacious drift;
Unappeasable cries of desolation—
Liable to fail;
Unalterable measure of insolence—
Loud snare;
Unsolicitable times of confusion—
Hideous despair;
Unrecognizable frames of aggression—
Formless roar;

Unattendable fears of grievance—
Horrid wails;
Unemcumberable tears of deprivations—
Free to scale;
Unanswerable preys of disingenuous—
Ever plotting;
Unpunishable sins of tyranny—
Altered impulses;
Unpreachable peace of calamity—
Life's rudiments;
Unexpressable sense of devotion—
Final rehearsal;
Unbelievable tale of transubstantive—
Prophetic sale;
Unspeakable fears of creation—
There will be.

All in Vain

I have been wondering; was our love
Made of words, laced with inchoate and
Throbbing needs?
Or was it the wreck of intentions—
Undeterred, and
Brooding deeds?
Is it possible that we fed on each other's
Unrests, covenant darkness,
That we spiraled ourselves
Into self-slaying without even noticing our
Mists of pain?
Or was it the pride to dismiss each other's
Disconsolate shivering but
To what gain?
I have been wondering, is our tomb sealed?
Are there things without end?

Preempted

I heard you once, your trembling cry—
Empty resonance;
Softly flung mournful tunes;
Your windless breath
Longing to be inhaled.

I touched you once, your weary lips—
Hushed to lull—
A strange swelling, then bereft;
Brittle strengths, unlocked knees
Longing soft persuasion.

I knew you once, so it began—
And also ended—
An unborn love, hastened away
I have been wandering since
Don't ask me where.

The Immigrant

Steeled in one dewy noon—
Autumnal winds;
Lured with the strange voices
Of passion and
The wildest eyes
I left for distant lands—
The music behind.
Tearless in the tangled wrecks
Of solitude; rusted,
In the youthful abyss
I pined for distant lands—
Without witness—
The sacred past left behind.

It Is Too Late

I didn't know
Your retreat
Stranded bare on earth
Your half-open lips
Lingering traces
Where you lay dying
Carved in a naked stone
Your ancient name
I remember now

Self-Deception

Please, lie to me.
Gray words at frail looks to a
Knife's edge—
Silent slain.

Please, brood stillness.
I don't know how to resurrect disembodied love;
Don't perfume your voice, nor
Sprinkle it with laughter;
Your mutinies are eye-deep.

Please, no need for signposts.
There are other debris to cross,
The field is unsown—
Tidings of plundered nest—
Is everything lost?

Please, do not worry.
Even my agony is imperfect, not worthy of your tears—
Unwilling myths.
I'll busy myself with our remnants of
Nocturnal gardens—
The final estrangement.

Unknown

Have I lost myself in light,
Walked asleep with truth
In plain sight?
Have I let my innocence die,
Unrestrained
With mortal wrongs?

Should I be blamed for want
Of a simple pain,
A calmer grief?
Should I let my past
Dissemble and render
Foreign songs?

Should I have known for sure
Who was I then, not just
Wandering cries?
Should I deepen my sorrow
Farther,
A vanished life?

Have I found my self in the dark,
Talked awake with lies, not so
Innocent ferocities?
Should I precipitate my demise
Guttural and real
Yet unknown?

Deserted

I marked the day she left
Trembling
It was early in the spring
Scentless
Not a single flower in bloom
No one has seen her again

I marked the sound as she left
Inaudible
It was early in the morning
Sunless
It was another mis-lamentation
Not a single tear in her eyes

I marked the thoughts as she left
Hell-bent
The familiar cast-away
Not a single mercy in her glance
No one has seen nor heard from her again

A Single Life

We didn't even know each other's name, but
Ready for the descent;
"Sex only rides hard," said he,—the unknown—"in
wilderness."
I put no faith in his stream of same, but
Didn't exactly lack anticipations.
"Sex only grows in dark", said he—the person—"in
Eagerness."
I felt, the fear lurking, but not
Without consent.
"Love also rides sex," said he—the guest—"in
Cooing;"
Where had I heard this? Wooing to barter! But,
I lost all my measures.
"Marriage rides sex" said he—the friend—"in
Kisses."
I seem to go from one empty home to another, but,
I wear my darkest pains, when alone.
"Sex rides sadness" said he—the lover—and
Proved tedious.

The Scent of Life

At the gains' end,
You must relent in your aim
Fiercely and
Be a hunter,
Where the remains are;
At the losses' end.
Take muted steps, and
Scent down the
Meaning of life.

Reluctant Silence

I live in lonely bounds
Even if it is above the brim
Forbidden inclinations
Unable to suppress
I don't know how to tell you this

I live in a disorderly mind;
It generates fear—
Molested brooding—
Unable to repress.

I live in a fearless edge;
It penetrates deep—
A daring fiction—
Unable to redress

I live in a forgotten meaning
Even if something beheld—
An aborted soul—
I don't know how to tell you this

Worthy of My Mind

I am not worthy of my mind
Full of counterfeit wisdoms, scattered songs
Altered in captivity—mad intent.

My mind dares to speak without restraint
Until all is bare, having mastered
Oblivion to all fears and leave
No trace of trespass—perilous impunity.

My mind doesn't starve for truth or offer
Respite for my repentances
It lives a life where everything is
Trivial, if not too insidious.

My mind is terror-driven, spread
Over the profane; it bares
Resemblance to all devourings
Faint reminiscence of redemption—too unreal.

The Death of Life

Day will not always follow the night
Soundless
Where do the suspicions grow, unrelenting,
In divination of truth or in delusions?—
False devotions.

The light will not always follow the dark
Fearful
Where do the innocents nest, enwombed?
Nobody wants to hear lamentations—
Ride of life.

Love will not always follow the hate
Frittered
Where do the illusions rove, unrepentant?
Nobody cares for the battle-bred—
Spent emotions.

Birth will not always follow death—
Honeyless combs.
Where do fallen heads rest, entombed
For distant faces, eyes and fists?—
Died of life.

A Poet

He is said to have been the last poet
Of importance who lived
In disharmony with his times.
He seemed forever angry and again, warring
Against himself.

He is said to have been noisily aged,
Spreading glooms of his choice but only
When he was not drunk.
He seemed invisibly violent as if warning
Against the rhyme.

He is said to have lacked the venom
Of melody, scaled the untempered,
When he was not sober.
He seemed to grow old and tedious,
Staining verses.

He is said to have written nothing at all
Unmeasured; disdained the tuneful disorder
When he was not a robber.
Though he had foresworn all these riles,
Someone should put an end
to his wiles.

Part III
I ELUDED LIFE

"Even on that last day, when the light of life departs, the wretches are not completely purged of all the taints, nor are they wholly freed of all the body's plagues. Down deep they harden fast—they must, so long engrained in the flesh—in strange, uncanny ways. And so the souls are drilled in punishment, they must pay for their old offenses. Some are hung splayed out, exposed to the empty winds, some are plunged in the rushing floods—their stains, their crimes scoured off or scorched away by fire."

Virgil, *The Aeneid*, Book VI
(Trans. by David West)

I Eluded Life

It is difficult to tell whether I suffer from
Depression or am simply bored out of my existence.
I convey a sense of calm, a
Dignified quiet. Meanwhile,
Hanging breathless on the verdict of saneness
By others.
I tell stories of misadventures, broken wings; is that lack of
Compassion or simply a scorn to grief?
I offer lascivious claims, ferocities of
Unhinged mind; but somehow keep banging on
Fragile dwellings with uninterested passion—
Love un-gifted.
I do not have a single lovely thought, real and lucid,
Just a vacant yearning for something that
I never had; days and nights seem blurred and endless—
Unwilling ears. But then,
I am not really eager to be heard or to hold
Dry tears.

My mind is not interested in before or afterness
The future has no memories, the past is ash-heap;
It lives outside of time and the meaning of all—
Bent on sedition. Why then, if
Nothing is nothing, everything hurts and leaves me with
No recourse.
They say I speak inaudibly, I've got nothing to say.
But that is a lie; I want to shout, drenched in sweat,
No one wants to tune to my voice or inhale my breath—
Dark flavored. How then
This is a life? Or is it simply death postponed deep in
My marrow?

The Taste of Ashes

All this was foretold
At no distant time
I'll cancel the earth and the skies
There'll be no more borders;
I'll bury myself in you,
Only clad with pain,
You'll rage and
Mutiny against my soul
Brand me with rusty nails and
Practice the art of hurting.
As the living curve rolls
At the end of endless,
I'll taste the ashes of
Undone years.

Yet, Why?

I often heard women in captivity
Wonder,
What life might be without their
Husbands.
Unkindled in their lukewarm beds,
Not to pretend to be breathless or blazing—
Hot spiced.
The longest nights.

Would fate be lenient if they
Escaped their neurotic dreads and traverse life
Impregnable?
Go all the way to its perilous edge—
Mad trance.
The envious nights.

But if there is no deliverance from the din
Of the unfortunate deed,
In full view,
Taking account of their fatal guiles in
Ascending numbers;
Banish their teeming thoughts—
In lashing tears.
The pernicious nights.

Ready-made Psyche

Let me not deceive you or
Myself.
A giant lid sitting on me
With a weird precision,
To muffle old songs
From scattering
The remnants of
False intoxications;
Not to lay bare all their secrets
At the remotest abysses.
There you have it; if not
Absolved by intention
I'll keep going down the same drift
With ready-made
Explanations.

Intended Tales

Tell me stories of our love that
Could be true if we existed—
Invent tales.
Did we dissolve in some disjointed dream,
Sought its lost content?
Did we dance to syllables of an unweeded song,
From unknown times and unworn places?
Who will remember all this?
There were no others.
Would love remember?—
If it existed—
Invent tales.

Bitter Rememberings

Here is one of my regrets:
Did I impute saintliness
To your lies?—
Domestic and virtuous;
Did I think you were
Too inert to sin?
Trivial affairs may be
A few vestiges of thought,
Much less traceable in deeds—
Seemingly escaped the rancid. So,
Let time decay our
Bitter rememberings.

Lull of Betrayal

I knew it was coming:
I noticed
Her eyes
Wasting truth.
She distilled silence
In that autumn of betrayal;
Bent the sun and
Burned maples orange
Lulled me tender.

Delirium

There were times I have forgotten
Your hurried pace;
Reticent to be in mine, or
In your own center; still yet
Your mildly covetous glances,
Bearing neither haunting nor
Joyful fears
Predestined to be left with
Unerring sadness;
Now, it no longer matters—
Dubious phrases.
To a chilling delirium
I cast all remembrance

I Don't
Want Man's Love

I don't want any man near
Presenting
Love-bearing sins;
Creeping into my holes
With their scented thorns, and
Cloying melodies
Of tyranny;
Repeated over and over
Till woven into me.
Their love is
Just endless breach and
Densely oblivious surges,
Unbroken with words.

Desultory Perdition

If I had to do it over
I wouldn't love women
With dry well and unmuted
Repose,
Hoarding thoughts of
Disdain;
Nor would I be tilted
In narrow lane,
Whispering
Constraint of plunder and
Succumb the heart's
Perdition.

The Ponderous

The Last night,
A null tumbled in and
Sealed her innocent lips—
To final aloneness.
Where is this weird conjunction?
I am left
With her cold ashes—
Crumbling to oblivion—
Steeped in self-pity,
Guilt, remorse, and
Throbs of self-accusations.
She is absolved
By death,
I am condemned to
To live.

Endurance

You only endured
My inebriated rage
Fast-falling into lust or
Hollowness,
Carrying inaudible tunes;
I, on the other hand,
Lived in terror
Of your tattered silence,
Carrying black incantations
In a pitch darkness

Intimidation of a Lover

If I said, we need to forget
Is grief mine?
There is a hardness in your eyes—
Unforgiving yawn;
If I said, our dream is torn
Is blame yours?
Can your love catch fire again?
Without melting down;
If I said ours are separate lusts
Is disunion right?
There is a hardness in your thighs—
Unresponsive sigh;
If I said ours are separate lives
To drift apart
Can the truth be told again?
Without wallow of hell.

If Once,
Why Not Again?

For once you loved me, I know
From my inmost core, no,
From your scent.
You don't love me anymore—
Coldest breath.

Then you needed me, I know
From my inward gaze, no,
From the color of your kiss.
You don't need me anymore—
Bruising smiles.

For now you want to leave me, I know
From my nameless dread, no,
From your pains.
You don't want me anymore—
Frozen gaze.

Premeditated
Forgiveness

You were the most confusing—
Of a few lovers I have known
Of course,
Of those retrievable—
By my time-kissed memory.
Casting aside your strays
Of desire, teeming
Yet unbroken—
Bereft beyond faithfulness;
You traversed inexpressible grounds—
Cried tuneless,
While our unchecked encounters
Grow only darker,
With each premeditated
Forgiveness.

Forsaken

I hear the dancing of church bells
God resigned;
I fall into the ethereal—
Indelible descent;
Is it to have forsaken the ardent or
The invisible?
I don't know how to mourn you.
I hear the chants where your grave lay—
Nightly sobs;
I fall into long-gone breathless kisses
Never calmer.
Is it to forsake the factious or
The secret longing?
I don't know how to mourn you.

The Second Chance

I wondered whether you were happy
You asked for nothing,
Only my time;
You flung your soul to
A sullen wall.
I wondered whether you got me right
When I was alive;
The nights have failed you
Every time.
You threw yourself to
Unscented thighs;
Now the journey is over,
I wonder whether you are happy
Do you ask for his time?
Do you fling your soul to
Stranger lips?
I wonder whether you get him right
When I lie under.

Inside of Time

In the principle of things—
Delivered line by line—
Will there be no meaning in
Mute symbols stamped on dust?
What else had I to do,
Yearn for the flavor
Of dirt, and
Inhale its scent?
Does that sound like
There is a point
Existing inside of time?

The Unreal World

I forgot the name of my last lover;
No, I didn't forget,
I just don't remember—
Bound to forlorn.
Of all things betrayed me
I want deliverance
From time;
From this swarming sense of
Oblivion, devouring sounds,
Light and darkness.
My placid claim that she is
Where old lovers wither
Doesn't alter the fact that
The world is unreal.

On a Par

Now, I have no name;
The one that I had
Far too long
Frayed around
The edges of time,
Obscuring present into
The cradle;
It nagged with me endless—
Litany of inordinate—
That much I remember,
On a par with all others.

Nameless

I do not live in myself, riding tide of others, in obscure lands
I am a ghost without sight who stammers through life
Scentless

I do not live in my time, leaving no footprints, in all times
I am a word without claim who baffles himself
Senseless

I do not sing for myself, being well-versed, beyond the
    edges
I am a hint without missive, who woos the blizzard
Restless

I do not know myself, denouncing the earthlings, dismissive
I am a carcass, who feebly wanders
No Address

I do not weep for myself, practicing smiles on adulterated
  ears
I am a mutation who pines for who never was
Ceaseless

I do not care for myself, unweaving grave, as if feeling
I am a time-spitted intruder who longs to be
Nameless

Beyond Remembering

I had one story and one story only
I could have told it better
Not necessarily from want,
From the earned age of truth, but
I wasn't worthy of it.
I played the trivial parts of
My own life
And poisoned its well;
Impersonated the joy and the despair,
Ate darkness, drank tears and
Disbelieved in vain.
There were too many notes,
Yet not enough;
Picked my own pockets and
Wildly guessed the loot.
Now that I feel the tug of parting—
Left no trace.

Had I been more loved or at least
Desired,
No god would have ever died.
Is that what I really meant?
That part of the whole
Is lost on me;
But now it matters not, for I am
Beyond remembering.

Virtual Death

I have been dead for a while, though,
Some thoughts of immunity
Or its similitude,
Until I acquired the envy of despair and
Resolved to declare: Unshackled at last!
It is the deliverance
From ache of being.

This is how my death began, undeserving
Then I got plunged (a blot?)
Into the depths of the endless,
Only broken by life.

It is scarcely known
Death dismembers time;
Now, is no longer now,
Then, was then;
There hovers only a sense of
Forever, in a brooding darkness.

An embalming noise clinging into my skin,
And the smell of it
Creeps into the taste of earth
In my mouth.

A new song woven into my muted voice,
Fear-scented,
"If ever I would die death"
There will be no plaintive whine
But, here I am; am I?
I only wonder not in a rueful way
Whether I have ever existed
In my virtual death.

Had I been more loved or at least
Desired,
No god would have ever died.
Is that what I really meant?
That part of the whole
Is lost on me;
But now it matters not, for I am
Beyond remembering.

Virtual Death

I have been dead for a while, though,
Some thoughts of immunity
Or its similitude,
Until I acquired the envy of despair and
Resolved to declare: Unshackled at last!
It is the deliverance
From ache of being.

This is how my death began, undeserving
Then I got plunged (a blot?)
Into the depths of the endless,
Only broken by life.

It is scarcely known
Death dismembers time;
Now, is no longer now,
Then, was then;
There hovers only a sense of
Forever, in a brooding darkness.

Fit to Die

I never found a satisfactory solution
For living, while fully sustaining my profound
Doubts. Tell me friends, how do you decipher
Unfamiliar tunes, separate out the coined love
From the counterfeit,
Without return?

I never found a satisfactory confusion
For being, while never exiled from the
Null. Tell me friends, how do you escape
Thorns of life and not hurl through
The long descent,
With no return?

Maybe my life is an inextricable error,
Shriveled in anxiety, drenched in tears;
Stripped off its unmelodious quarrels,
Simply an empty want in its sorrow.
Still less resolved: when is the parting time,
And the place for the unfit for life
With a certitude of sense to yield
Fit to die?

Time Slayed

When I die, I want to die
An unadulterated death;
To feel it all with
Sober prelude of foreknowledge,
And coloring—
Free from the old and sequestered
Norms of
Self-devoted sympathy. Because
I simply existed within a song
Anyway,
Time interdicted and
Slayed it;
Leaving me inordinately
Bereft,
For fear that I might not die or
Refuse to live
Where gods worship man.

I Don't Want to Live

I cannot sleep
My eyes are glued
On my forehead;
I cannot breathe
My nose is clogged
With harsh scents of defiled;
I cannot eat
My stomach is full
With remnants of fear;
I cannot speak
My lips open only
To cry and moan;
I cannot hear
My ears hear only
Voices without sound;
I cannot move
Parts of my body are heaped,
Loathed and interred;

I cannot live
My heart, my mind, my soul are
Too slowly falling into decay;
I don't want to be
Anymore.

Haunted

This is what haunts me:
What if songs be trapped
In deafness;
The colors and the kisses
Sprinkled no more
Over the flesh of laughter;
What if uninhabited wombs remain
Immaculate—
Empty tombs of love—
Not even remembering their sins.
This is what really haunts me:
Never to be again.

Perpetual Surprise

There was a time, not too long ago
I held a lascivious claim
Over valley and mountains,
Palaces and tawdry houses.
I dared to undertow
Sonnets of truths, and half-truths
Unrehearsed.
I fiddled with virgins and whores—
Dry eyes and roaring deafness—
Wild, lucid and colossal calm;
Now I am resigned to recesses
Of my remembrances,
Even forgiveness
Chisels my nerves;
Where I weep in
Perpetual surprise.

I Am Not in My Place

My heart is not in its place, in fact,
Far out of sight;
How could it come to that descent
To preserve its warped pain?

My lips are not in their place, in fact
Drifted away apart;
How could they come to that agony
To dissolve an intransigent desire?

My eyes are not in their place, in fact,
Plucked out of their duet of tears;
How could they come to that arrest
To practice their growth of death?

If

If I had known that I am dying
I could have delivered
Unborn moments,
I would not have tried to make right
All my wrongs,
Definitely not be overwrought
Upon my lived hours.

If I had known that I am alive
I could have interred
Midnight torments;
I would not have tried to outflank
All my fears,
Definitely not expect to be
Absolved by dying.

The Graveyard

This is where the dead keep their bones
I know, I was there;
This is where divined stories sleep
In the darkness of throne, earth murmurs
Without lips.
This is where the palest breezes whisper
In the coldness of inner shrine
Without sound.
This is where the fairest nights slumber
In the dimness of waning stars
Without color.
This is where the loftiest grave sinks
In the eternal ruins
Without time.
This is where the remotest star blinks
In the boundless canopy
Without space.

This is where the sublime smiles freeze
In the ethereal harmony
I know I was there.
This is where the dead eat their bones.

This Is How I Want Myself Sung Of

He always smiled
Through his misty eyes
Whispered aloud
A soaring silence

He wanted to see love
In the gleam of others' eyes
As if he didn't care
Clumsiest disguise

He conveyed a sense of quiet
The fiercest unrest
Fought to surrender
The salvation lost

He walked the line, sort of
Hollowing out
Hurled himself into women
Piercing lamentations

He reined in his worst quests
Unholy ruthless
Chiseled the nerves
Hanging in breathless

He rendered the magic
Riddled reckless
Wronged the moist and the dry
Virginal darkness

He fiddled with life
Across forgiveness
Plundered sleeping thighs
In tearful hours

He enchanted broken wings
rehearsed wonderment
deserted the mistaken
pinkish eyes

He resigned to his recesses
deep in his marrow
quarried zest of all
sonnet of lies

He told stories of hindered mind
faithless fables
traveled furtively
riding the barren time

He hushed his lonely descent
tumbled to decay
decanted his soul
and banished yonder

He was never here anyway
a few empty trickles
were stilled before, deathless
now beyond remembering

Final Throes

I have been waiting for this moment:
To be beyond yearning;
To take my leave from verse—
The meaning of it strives—
Kneel down and slay it to prose,
Scatter its devouring words
Over the poet's grave.
The final throes
Almost within reach;
To wrap myself in silence and lower it
To the infinite descent,
Pitiless name
As it began and so it ends, yet
Still the same.